NOT *of* THIS WORLD

JOURNEY TO THE SECRET PLACE

ANDREY SHAPOVAL

Table of Contents

Introduction 1

Day 1   The Secret Place of the Most High 5

Day 2   Be Still and Know 15

Day 3   His Voice is in His Presence 27

Day 4   His Guidance is in His Voice 39

Day 5   Read Until the Word Speaks to You 49

Day 6   The Power of Praise 57

Day 7   Arm Yourself! 67

Day 8   The Seven Spirits of God 79

Day 9   Fight for Hunger 91

Day 10   Father's Will 101

Introduction

I RECEIVED A COMMENT ON ONE of my sermons once. It said, "I'm setting a goal to get closer to God this coming year." As I read it, I thought, "It won't work..." Even though this is a fantastic goal, achieving it becomes difficult because the goal is vague. Moreover, how would someone gauge if they go closer to God by the end of that year? It's impossible. Thus, I propose a different approach to achieving spiritual growth. Let's outline practical steps and actions that can be taken every day. For example, "I'm setting a goal to get up half an hour earlier every day to spend time with God. Because of this, I will be closer to God by the end of next year." Your goals should be practical, precise, and measurable. For example: set aside at least 30 minutes daily to spend quality time in the Word and prayer, separate one day each month to be alone with God, and fast for one day (or a few days) every month. By adding these practices to your daily schedule, you will see a noticeable transformation in your spiritual growth, a deeper connection with the Holy Spirit, and an enhanced ability to discern His voice and guidance.

In this journal, I want to lead you step by step into the secret place to show you how to practically apply the truths I've shared in the book "*Not of This World*." I hope to ignite the desire for intimacy with God in you so you may experience the joy of a relationship with Him. Together, we will work on developing the discipline of coming to the secret place, listening to God, and continuously growing in Him. This journal contains messages for each day, Scriptures to memorize, questions for personal reflection, tips, and practical application. By consistently completing these daily exercises, you will deepen your connection with God, become more sensitive to the presence of God, and learn how to hear His voice and come under His lordship.

As you go through this journal, set aside time to be alone with God and listen to what He will say within you (see Habakkuk 2:1-2 NLT). Start recording whatever the Holy Spirit tells you in the secret place; even if it's one word, write it down. Short notes are powerful, too. Train yourself to pause and tune in to His voice, then write down or draw what you see, hear, and grasp in your secret place. Do not skip that part of the journal. Use the writing section to record what He reveals to you. And most importantly, enjoy His presence while letting Him enjoy yours.

If you miss a day, don't go through two chapters the following day. Don't try to read through the whole journal in one sitting either—the point is not to finish the journal quickly but to develop a consistent habit of abiding in His Word and growing in relationship with Him day after day. Cultivate a daily habit of withdrawing to be alone with

God. Persevere, and you will soon notice how you more clearly hear His voice and become more aware of both the Holy Spirit's presence guidance.

God is waiting for you in the secret place. Are you ready to meet with Him?

Then, let's get started.

The Secret Place of the Most High

Day 1

Psalm 91

¹ He who dwells in the secret place of the Most High shall abide under the shadow of the Almighty.

² I will say of the Lord, "He is my refuge and my fortress; my God, in Him I will trust."

³ Surely He shall deliver you from the snare of the fowler and from the perilous pestilence.

⁴ He shall cover you with His feathers, and under His wings you shall take refuge; His truth shall be your shield and buckler.

⁵ You shall not be afraid of the terror by night, nor of the arrow that flies by day,

⁶ Nor of the pestilence that walks in darkness, nor of the destruction that lays waste at noonday.

⁷ A thousand may fall at your side, and ten thousand at your right hand; but it shall not come near you.

⁸ Only with your eyes shall you look, and see the reward of the wicked.

⁹ Because you have made the Lord, who is my refuge, even the Most High, your dwelling place,

¹⁰ No evil shall befall you, nor shall any plague come near your dwelling;

¹¹ For He shall give His angels charge over you, to keep you in all your ways.

¹² In their hands they shall bear you up, lest you dash your foot against a stone.

¹³ You shall tread upon the lion and the cobra, the young lion and the serpent you shall trample underfoot.

¹⁴ "Because he has set his love upon Me, therefore I will deliver him; I will set him on high, because he has known My name.

¹⁵ He shall call upon Me, and I will answer him; I will be with him in trouble; I will deliver him and honor him.

¹⁶ With long life I will satisfy him, and show him My salvation."

I RENTED A CABIN IN THE woods once to be alone with God for a few days. I wanted it to be away from all the commotion and distractions of everyday life. This little cabin was nestled deep in the forest next to a river, making it the perfect spot for me to worship and read the Word. As soon as I arrived, I grabbed my guitar and Bible and headed to the river to worship and read the Word. Not a soul was around, only the beauty of nature and fresh air. After a few hours, the sun began to set, and I started hearing sounds coming from the woods around me. Soon, I started hearing the wailing of an unknown creature, the howling of the wind, and creaking resembling a rusty swing… I built a fire and continued to worship God.

At some point, I thought, "Okay, that's enough nature for today. I'm going back inside the house. I'd rather read the Bible there." The darkness seemed to deepen instantly as soon as I put out the fire. The eerie sounds intensified, creating an atmosphere straight out of a horror movie. I started walking fast. Then faster. Then, even faster. I started full-on sprinting with my guitar in one hand and my Bible in the other hand. I finally reached the house, hurriedly found the key, flung open the door, and bolted into the house. I was totally out of breath. My heart was pounding. At least I was safe. There, I opened the Bible and started reading, but I couldn't focus on what I was reading. What a letdown! I kept hearing unsettling, wild screams, rustling, and cracking noises. Relaxing was impossible.

I was disappointed and disheartened. I had come to present myself to the Lord and spend quality time with Him, but fear took such a hold of me that my focus was gone. My attention was consumed with what was happening around my cabin in the woods. Each loud noise only increased my fear, making it impossible to find the stillness I sought. That night, I spent more time gripped by fear than time with God. With a heavy heart, I made a decision, "I'll go to sleep. There's no point in me staying awake anyway. I can't even concentrate on the Scripture." Despite my efforts, I couldn't fall asleep either. I tossed and turned all night, haunted by these eerie sounds and screams that kept stressing me out. It became clear that retreats in the woods weren't my thing. I didn't want to be there anymore. What was the point of all this if I couldn't concentrate on God? I decided to leave as soon as the sun came up.

Waking up the following day, it was so beautiful and peaceful around me: the sun was radiant, and the air was warm, carrying a refreshing breeze. The songs of birds filled the air, and the river was flowing, only adding to the peaceful atmosphere. "Well," I thought, "Since I'm already here and this is such a calming and inspiring atmosphere, I'll just go to the riverbank again, worship God, and read the Word. Then, in the afternoon, before dark, I'll drive back home." I was about to leave, then I stopped. "Wait, where are my keys?" I frantically looked for them everywhere, trying to remember where I left them. They were nowhere to be found. I was in such a rush last night. Where did I leave them after opening the door?

I remembered the fear that gripped me last night, so I started to pray while searching for the keys, "Lord, deliver me from all fear and anxiety. I don't want it!!!" *But where could the keys be?* I couldn't find them anywhere; it was so frustrating. Eventually, I decided to stop wasting time and go without the keys. Walking out, I saw my keys sticking out of the door lock outside. What on earth?! I was in such a panic the previous night that I didn't even realize I had left the keys in the lock when I opened the door. They stayed in the door all night. Can you imagine?

When I saw them, I broke out laughing, and at that moment, God began speaking to me. His presence enveloped me. I laughed and cried and heard God all at the same time, "Son, do you realize now that it is I Who protects you! If someone wanted to come and harm you, they could have done so effortlessly. You helped them by leaving the keys outside. Do you understand what I'm showing you? Let Me make it clear to you: I'm your Lord, your shield and protection. Your keys don't protect you; I do. Even if you forget your keys outside, no one will come near your dwelling because I have set you apart for Myself. You are Mine. I will protect you and cover you. I'm showing you now that you're under the shadow of the Almighty. So, calm down and breathe freely!" He revealed to me the depth of His lordship over my life, assuring me of His constant protection in every step I take.

At that moment, Psalm 91 was revealed to me in a new light—the power of our covenant with the Lord as we grow under His lordship. This psalm is a blueprint of God's lordship in our life:

> *He who dwells in the secret place of the Most High shall abide under the shadow of the Almighty. I will say of the Lord, "He is my refuge and my fortress; my God, in Him I will trust." (Psalm 91:1-2).*

The one who *dwells* in the secret place of the Most High is the one who is under His complete protection. Friend, it is not enough to come into His presence only from time to time, only when necessary, or only on Sundays or holidays—you must **dwell** under His lordship, His authority, and in His Kingdom.

Did I leave the woods after that night? No, I stayed. I believe that in the moment by the door when I was overwhelmed by God's presence, I got delivered from all fear! Amidst my laughter and tears, I received freedom!

When the next night came, I was in my cabin, absorbed in reading His Word. The fear truly left me. It was amusing to hear the barking, howling, cracking, and screeching around my cabin in the woods. The sounds no longer frightened me; instead, I felt His peace and strong presence with Me—I was under the shadow of the Almighty, dwelling in the secret place of the Most High. I was no longer afraid of these terrors by night. It's fascinating how the first and second nights went so differently; one was full of fear, and the other was filled with His glory and peace!

During that retreat in the forest, I witnessed a prophetic picture of the days ahead—for some, it will be a time filled with terror and dread, while for others, it will be a time of greatness and glory! In the last days, the difference will be clearly shown between those who are under His lordship and those who are not. When He is your Lord, the most challenging thing you would have to face is seeing the events unfolding in the world outside your window.

You see, when you live under His lordship, you live in a house built on a different foundation, the Father's house; you rest under His protection, not because you deserve it, *but because you made the Lord, who is my refuge, even the Most High, your dwelling place, No evil shall befall you, nor shall any plague come near your dwelling; for He shall give His angels charge over you, to keep you in all your ways. In their hands they shall bear you up, lest you dash your foot against a stone* (Psalm 91:9-12).

That's a fantastic description of the model of God's lordship. Note that Psalm 91 is divided into two parts. The first half reveals what God will do to those who live under His lordship: He will protect and provide for them. The second half explains why He protects and provides for them. When you know you are protected and have provision under His lordship, your attention shifts from seeking answers for your fears and needs to fulfilling His will! To accomplish His assignment, He gives you power and authority to trample on snakes and scorpions. Under His lordship, you will not sit idle, you will take action, you will trample on the lion and the cobra, the young lion and the serpent (see Psalm 91:13).

And in the final verse of Psalm 91, God promises:

> *With long life, I will satisfy him and show him My salvation* (Psalm 91:16).

Wow! Take a moment to meditate on this promise: if your future is horrible and scary, filled with sickness, poverty, and suffering — then a long life wouldn't be a blessing, would it? That is why intimacy with God and obedience to His voice are essential to all of us—Obedience lets God lead you into a long and *blessed* life under the shadow of the Almighty!

Friend, we need to grow under the lordship of God and fully devote ourselves to Him. Remember, **when He is your Lord, He will take care of your needs so that you can focus on His will.**

Reflection:

Take a moment to reflect: Do you experience fear, anxiety, or panic attacks? If the answer is yes, then that area of your life is not fully surrendered to His lordship. The Scripture says, *"And you shall know the truth, and the truth shall make you free"* (John 8:32). It's time to deal with and overcome those fears.

Begin by identifying the fear holding you back, writing it down, and confronting it in prayer. Name the fear and command it to get out of your life; then, declare the truth of God's Word and His promises into those areas occupied by fear.

_____

_____

_____

_____

_____

_____

Activation:

Spend the next 15 minutes praying in tongues and then another 15 minutes in stillness, abiding in His presence. I practice it this way: I pray in the Spirit freely, then pause and wait silently. I start meditating on His Word and focus my thoughts on Him. As I do this, I attentively listen to the Holy Spirit within me. Listen to His voice in the quiet of your secret place and wait patiently to see what the Lord says, shows, or reveals within your spirit.

Now, write down what you felt, heard, or saw.

_____

_____

_____

_____

_____

_____

_____

_____

_____

_____

_____

_____

_____

_____

_____

_____

_____

_____

_____

Be Still and Know

Day 2

Psalm 45

To the Chief Musician. A Psalm of the sons of Korah. A Song for Alamoth.

¹ God *is* our refuge and strength, a very present help in trouble.

² Therefore we will not fear, even though the earth be removed, and though the mountains be carried into the midst of the sea;

³ *Though* its waters roar *and* be troubled, *though* the mountains shake with its swelling. *Selah*

⁴ *There is* a river whose streams shall make glad the city of God, the holy *place* of the tabernacle of the Most High.

⁵ God *is* in the midst of her, she shall not be moved; God shall help her, just at the break of dawn.

⁶ The nations raged, the kingdoms were moved; He uttered His voice, the earth melted.

⁷ The Lord of hosts *is* with us; the God of Jacob *is* our refuge. *Selah*

⁸ Come, behold the works of the Lord, Who has made desolations in the earth.

⁹ He makes wars cease to the end of the earth; He breaks the bow and cuts the spear in two; He burns the chariot in the fire.

¹⁰ Be still, and know that I *am* God; I will be exalted among the nations, I will be exalted in the earth!

¹¹ The Lord of hosts is with us; the God of Jacob *is* our refuge. *Selah*

I HAVE ALWAYS BEEN EAGER TO understand how God thinks, what His original plan was, how He envisioned our relationships, and what I need to pay attention to so I can draw closer to Him. I want to know His ways, not just His works. I've spent many hours studying and meditating on Scripture to find answers to my questions. His original design of relationship with man is found in the book of Genesis:

The Lord God planted a garden eastward in Eden, and there He put the man whom He had formed (Genesis 2:8).

The word "Eden"[1] in Hebrew is depicted by five strokes, and each one has a special meaning: "spot," "moment," "open door," "presence," and "delightful place." In other words, Eden was not just a physical garden; it was a spot on earth in a moment when the presence of God was an open door to heaven. Essentially, God created man and placed him in His presence. The man had direct communion with God under an open heaven, and the presence of God remained with the man. Therefore, Eden was not just a physical garden but a spiritual environment.

God's original plan was for His children to live in His presence. From His presence, where the heavens were connected to the earth, man could rule the earth, have dominion, be fruitful, multiply, and spread Eden, or the Kingdom of God, throughout the whole world until the presence of God filled the entire earth. As this was God's original idea, it's imperative to prioritize His presence above all else. We can accomplish everything from His presence by dwelling in the secret

---

1   Myles Munroe, https://www.youtube.com/watch?v=9NmgNUAxFNw (accessed 25.07.2023); likewise, see Darrell Parsons, *Release Your Words – Impact Your World: Let Your Voice Be Heard!* Parsons Publishing House 2008, pg. 78

place of the Most High and carrying His presence wherever we go. Then, in all our ways, we will be successful and able to fulfill His will.

How do we practically apply these principles and establish them in our lives?

In Chapter 3 of my book, *Not of this World*, I covered the structure of God's Temple. In the Old Covenant, it served as a place where the glory of God dwelt on earth. The Temple's design carries prophetic symbolism, showing us the various levels of intimacy we can have with God. It unveils the steps to draw near Him, starting with the outer courts, moving through the inner courts, and finally entering the Holy of Holies. The Holy of Holies was the manifest presence of God. In the Old Testament, only the high priest had the privilege to enter there, and even he could only do so once a year. But in the New Testament, because of the sacrifice of Jesus Christ, we have access to the manifest presence of God, the Holy of Holies, under His lordship.

I won't repeat what I've already discussed in the book. Instead, I will show you how to go deeper into the presence of God and enter the Holy of Holies. Yes, this process is a journey, and there are requirements you must meet to go from the outer courts to the inner courts and further into the Holy of Holies, where you fully surrender yourself to the Lord and come face to face with Him.

Perhaps you're thinking, "Face to face with the Lord? I don't know if this is possible for me." Well, that's why you're holding this journal—so that communion with the Lord and intimacy with Him becomes your reality. Without experiencing it for yourself, you will not understand the depth of His presence and what it means to know

God. In the depth of His presence, you join yourself with His Spirit, get to know the Lord and the process of adoption will take place. If you are hesitant or unwilling to venture deeper into the Holy of Holies, your relationship with Him will remain superficial and based on theory, information, and other people's experiences.

To know God personally, we must learn to enter the depth of His presence. His presence is more than just a physical sensation you may experience during a worship song or a prayer. Some people think that goosebumps are a sign of God's presence. This is only partially accurate. The levels of His presence are much more profound. I'm talking about the level where you are immersed in His rest, shalom, and complete peace and where the harmony of spirit, soul, and body happens. So, how do we get there? Psalm 46:10 says:

> *Be still, and know that I am God; I will be exalted among the nations, I will be exalted in the earth!*

"Be still" in the English dictionary refers to silence and motionlessness. In other words, you must turn off and let go of EVERYTHING. This includes quieting your physical body.

"Be still and know" is talking about stopping in a way where all other things fade from your sight. To be still with God is to set aside a time and place when you leave everything behind and give all your attention to the Lord. That means there should no longer be room for a phone, computer, messages, books, or social media. You can't bring anything in with you.

When you share the secret place of the Most High with other things, you're placing them on the same level as God, allowing these things to interrupt you and giving them great importance. In such settings, He will not reveal His heart to you. I've often noticed that people pray, worship, and sing to God but never put their phones away and constantly check them. Let's be honest; your phone is not the problem. The problem is your soul being so attached to your phone. If you cannot disconnect from the phone or your cares, thoughts, plans, and feelings during time alone with God, He will not share His heart with you. He won't reveal Himself and speak to you when your attention is divided. God won't lower Himself. He knows His worth far too well to share His thoughts with someone who doesn't give Him their full attention. You should act appropriately if you say He is your Lord and King. That means you must consciously choose to remove everything that could distract you.

When God turns His attention, gaze, and breath on you, there should be no room for anything else. He will reveal Himself only when 100% of the attention is on Him. I'll say more; some might not understand this yet, but you need to learn to go deeper in the presence of God and further to the point that you even turn off the worship music—all other voices must be silent before Him. Nothing but His presence should have our full attention.

In the Holy place or the inner court of the Temple, the Levites led services with music and singing. However, when the high priest entered the Holy of Holies, he did so alone! The high priest entered without any musical accompaniment or the presence of the Levites. The Holy of Holies was the very presence of God. He stepped in there with a rope tied to his leg, which was connected to him in case he died in God's presence so that the other priests could pull him out of there.

The rope symbolizes the complete surrender of self before entering. It's important to emphasize this truth again: if you want to enter the depth of His presence, everything around you must lose its allure. If you yearn for His presence and desire His attention, disconnect yourself from the world's distractions and wholeheartedly focus on Him.

In the Holy place, you create the conditions necessary to enter the Holy of Holies. Look for ways that will enable you to enter God's presence. Many turn on worship music, pray in tongues, and sing praises to enter God's presence. All those things are good, but when you connect with God and feel His hand on you, go deeper into a place where you even close the door to the things that helped you get there. EVERYTHING around you should be silent, and EVERYTHING within you should be quiet, too.

God taught me this lesson during one of my mountain retreats. The Holy Spirit said, "To go deeper into My presence and behold My glory, turn off everything, silence the music, voices, and everything else that can obstruct My communication with you." That's why I'm sharing this with you. If you want to go deeper into the heart of God and start seeing far, high, deep, and wide, then close the door to everything around you and inside you. Turn off absolutely everything that could distract you, calm your feelings, emotions, and thoughts, and enter divine peace. This practice holds great importance. Only when you are still can you hear His voice.

What does stillness in prayer mean? I remember God once told me, "I don't want to talk with your emotions when you are overwhelmed. I want to talk to the real you, your spirit. It is your responsibility to calm your soul and body so that you can hear Me." The next thing

God said, "Learn not only to calm your emotions; learn to still your body." Yes, we sometimes walk when we pray. Most often, it's during intercession prayer or prayer in tongues. But to behold His glory and go deeper, you must learn to be still physically, emotionally, and mentally. Your body should also calm down and align with your spirit and soul. In that moment, you let go of everything and focus on God, for you are entering the Holy of Holies. And in that depth of His presence, you no longer talk. You surrender yourself entirely to Him. You're not there to pray in tongues; you're there to listen to God. It's not just silence; it's embracing the depth of silence. To "be still" means to enter the depth of this tranquility and peace.

Sometimes, when I spend time alone with Him on retreats, I enter a state where I can feel myself sinking into some kind of vacuum, a different dimension, immersing somewhere deep where His presence and glory cover me. Everything that used to make noise and rattle in the background fades away. I no longer hear anything else around me. It's like being in a barrel, closed from the outside world. All my attention is on Him. In such a state, you hear God and begin to understand Him, His thoughts, and His words. You begin to understand what He wants to say, and you don't hear it—you understand it. You understand what He's showing you. You understand what He's revealing to you. You *understand*. It's the language of the spirit. That's how the spiritual world talks. That's how God talks, which is why it's sometimes hard to find the right words to describe it.

His voice doesn't come through sound but through thoughts, images, understandings, and impressions. God does not speak like a human. This means His voice needs to be understood, realized, and discerned.

I am often asked:

"Andrey, how do you hear God?"

"I understand what He's saying to me in the moment. I may not always hear His exact words, but I understand what He wants to say."

"How do you develop this understanding?"

"Through practice, by allowing the Holy Spirit to immerse you into His presence."

Start practicing what I teach you here, and you will start understanding His voice and Word.

Let me point out: I'm not talking about prophecy or a prophetic gift but about getting to know God and having an intimate relationship with Him. The prophetic gift can work even when you are in a commotion. But when you want God to reveal Himself to you and build intimacy with Him, put an end to all the commotion and quiet your soul and body to connect with Him. Present yourself to the Lord and spend time with Him to know Him and to get to know His voice. Some might say, "That sounds complicated. I don't have time for that." Well, maybe that's why you don't know His voice. God always speaks to your spirit. Can you bring your feelings, thoughts, emotions, soul, and body to rest so that His voice can reach from the realm of the spirit into your spirit in a language that will become understandable to you?

Don't pass on to God things that you have to do:

- God will not quiet your emotions — you must quiet them yourself.

- God will not silence your feelings — you must silence them yourself.

- God will not turn off your phone — you must set it aside.

- God will not force your attention on Him — you must direct it on Him yourself.

And finally, when everything that distracted your attention has faded, you have entered a state of divine peace. In this condition, you won't want to keep your eyes open, and you're not talking anymore. You leave yourself entirely to Him. It's His turn to speak. So, close your eyes and see. See what He's showing you. Listen to what He's saying. See what He reveals to you.

Reflection:

Make an honest analysis: what things have the most power over your soul and distract your attention when you set aside time to pray and be with God? Take a moment to reflect on everything that can take your attention away from Him. To go deep into His presence, you must learn to disconnect from those things.

Write it down: what takes your attention away when you want to focus entirely on Him?

_____

_____

_____

_____

_____

_____

_____

_____

_____

Activation:

Spend the next 15 minutes praying in tongues and then another 15 minutes waiting in silence and stillness in His presence. Listen attentively to His voice in the quiet of your secret place and wait to see what the Lord says, shows, or reveals inside your spirit. Record everything you hear and see:

_____

_____

_____

_____

_____

_____

_____

_____

_____

_____

_____

_____

_____

_____

His Voice is in His Presence

Day 3

Psalm 23

A Psalm of David.

[1] The LORD *is* my shepherd; I shall not]want.

[2] He makes me lie down in green pastures; He leads me beside the still waters.

[3] He restores my soul; He leads me in the paths of righteousness for His name's sake.

[4] Yea, though I walk through the valley of the shadow of death, I will fear no evil; for You are with me; Your rod and Your staff, they comfort me.

[5] You prepare a table before me in the presence of my enemies; You anoint my head with oil; my cup runs over.

[6] Surely goodness and mercy shall follow me all the days of my life; and I will dwell in the house of the Lord forever.

PSALM 23 DESCRIBES THE ESSENCE of the lordship of God. David, the author of this song, asserts His faith in God. This isn't his proclamation or prayer. This is the way of life under the full lordship of God.

From the beginning, David doesn't say, "God is my Shepherd"; he says, "The LORD is my Shepherd." We already discussed the difference between 'God' and 'LORD' in the book. David knew that difference, too. In this Psalm, he doesn't share his heart towards the Lord, but the Lord's heart towards him! In other words, David acknowledges his love for God and his submission to His lordship, and he says, "I love Him and allow His lordship to rule over me; and in return, these are the blessings He bestows upon me! All I have in my life comes from the Lord!"

The verse *"He makes me to lie down in green pastures"* speaks of provision. The Lord prepared green pastures for those who live under His lordship, and He has life and life more abundantly prepared for us. That's where He wants to lead us.

"He leads me beside the still waters"—speaks of finding rest in God. The Holy Spirit yearns to immerse us in peace, enabling us to attune our ears to His gentle whispers. Why is water mentioned in this context? Water satisfies our thirst, brings comfort, symbolizes life, and represents the Holy Spirit. People never get tired of looking at fire and water—these are a few personifications of God's nature. The Holy Spirit wants to lead us beside still waters, bringing us into the harmony of spirit, soul, and body, and from that place of rest, teach us and lead us into the will of God.

"He leads me in the paths of righteousness for His name's sake"—speaks of the leading of the Holy Spirit, who leads us when we are under His lordship. He guides us into fulfilling God's purpose in our lives, bringing about His will on earth. As we walk on these paths of righteousness, He commands the angels concerning you (see Psalm 91:11). On these paths of righteousness, He guides, protects, brings provision, resolves situations, supplies our needs, and considers everything we do to fulfill His will.

Take a closer look at the sequence in these verses:

1. Makes me lie down in green pastures,

2. Leads me beside the still waters,

3. Restores my soul,

4. Leads me in paths of righteousness.

Let's recap: He wants to lead us to green pastures and still waters, where our mind, soul, and body can find true peace. From this place of rest, He guides us with His voice. These are the principles that God taught David: when you are at rest, you will begin to hear His voice within you clearly; He will guide you personally and send you from His presence to do His will.

Why is this order important? And why is dwelling in His presence essential? Because His voice is in His presence. Of course, God can speak to us from the outside or through other people. However, He does not want to guide you through other people. God draws you back to the secret place into a personal relationship with Him through other people. He wants to teach you to hear His voice and listen to Him yourself, not depend on others to hear Him for you. God speaks from the outside to get your attention; His intentions are clear: He wants to lead you personally, not through others. Let me emphasize again that from the outside, the Holy Spirit will stop you and warn you, but it's not His primary method of leading you. Warning is not the same as leading. He desires to guide you personally. That is why you must learn to stop, be still in His presence, and listen to Him. And the more you obey His voice, the more He can manifest His lordship in your life.

When I realized this truth, I began creating the environment to enter His rest so that nothing would distract me from spending time with God. As I've mentioned, you can walk around the room, play worship music, speak the Word, and pray in tongues as you enter His presence. All these steps lead you deeper: from the outer courts to the inner courts and only then to the Holy of Holies. You go there in stages, but when you enter the Holy of Holies, it becomes your Eden—your spot and moment with God where the heavens are open and He covers you with His glory.

As I mentioned in my book, I started a monthly practice of retreats with God in the mountains. I discovered the beauty of entering His rest (the Holy of Holies), where the depth of the Word began to be revealed to me. In that place, the Scripture would start to open, and sometimes, I even received a specific task from Him that I needed to do. The Holy Spirit led me through His voice. I remember once, I was in the mountains, spending time with God. When I go on such retreats, I try to choose a hotel with a sauna. The thing is, when I'm on retreats, I sit still, reading the Word and sitting in His presence for hours on end. Sometimes, my body gets numb, and every muscle in me starts to ache, so I like to go to the sauna to relax. After spending some time there, I returned to my room to be with the Lord. The sauna has become an integral part of my retreats with God.

And so, one day, I was in worship, and the deep presence of God enveloped me. I was in His glory, in the Holy of Holies. Suddenly, in this stillness, I hear God saying, "Go to the sauna." I thought, "What? Sauna? What does it mean? Maybe God is talking about being washed by the Word like the apostle Paul wrote in Ephesians?" And so, I started to meditate on that Scripture. Suddenly, I heard again, "Just go to the sauna." And I saw the sauna in my mind's eye. I've had similar experiences before when God would send me out of His presence to do His will (I've written about it in other books). Therefore, I understood that there was a mission God was giving me; He wanted to do something in the sauna.

I should mention that when I come out of that kind of stillness in the presence of God, I am susceptible to every sound and movement. Everything is too loud. If someone is next to me, I can hear how loudly they breathe. Maybe it sounds strange, but when you consciously put away absolutely every distraction for long periods of time, you start to notice every little thing. Honestly, it's difficult for me to switch quickly from that reality to the physical one.

So, while still in that hyper-sensitive state, I took my shorts and went down to the 3rd floor to find the sauna. I went in, and no one was there. "Well, there you go. Did I mix something up? Maybe it was the voice of my flesh, not the Holy Spirit? Why is no one here?" Since I was already there, I turned up the heat and sat down. Shortly after, the door opened, and a man came in. He was prominent in stature and was breathing heavily. His pace seemed a little off. He was either a little drunk or was struggling to move due to the heat I had set in the sauna.

The man sat down and was the first to speak:

"So, how much money did you lose down there?"

The thing is, there was a big casino on the hotel's bottom floor. That is likely why the prices at that hotel were lower than others; the hotel bet on visitors spending their money in the casino.

I replied:

"I don't gamble, and I don't play in casinos."

"Oh really? Then what are you doing here?"

"I'm spending time with God."

My answer caught him off guard. First, I didn't play casino like everyone else (or most people) there. Secondly, I was spending my time with God. And thirdly, I was talking about God, something he definitely didn't expect to hear in sauna. The man scratched his head and said with a grin:

"And what did God tell you?"

"You won't believe it. He said to come here."

He laughed and asked, "Why?"

"Probably because of you. He sent me here for you."

"For me?"

"Yes, He loves you very much and probably sees something that you're dealing with, suffering with, thinking about, and asking Him about... So, God took me out of prayer and brought me to the sauna so that you would ask me, and I would give you an answer."

Then this man sharply blurted out:

"There's no God! This is all nonsense!"

"You can say whatever you want. But I'm telling you what God told me. You're probably dealing with something, and He cares about you. That's why He told me to come here."

Then I received a word of knowledge and started giving him details about his back pain and problems in his marriage.

The man laughed and denied it, acting like he didn't care. Apparently, everything was fine. After that, we didn't talk much and sat there in silence. "I guess I've already said what God wanted me to say..." I walked out of the sauna with that thought. On my way to the room, he caught up with me, putting his shirt on while saying:

"Come to my car."

I looked at him, surprised, "What's this all of a sudden?"

Then he began pleading with me:

"Please, come with me."

"Why?"

"I'll explain later."

We went outside and sat in his old pickup truck. In the car, he explained that he and his wife were on the verge of divorce and had other family problems. Then he told me a long list of his illnesses and that he lived in constant unbearable back pain. Back in the sauna, I had a word of knowledge about all that. However, he faked being okay when I asked him about it in the sauna. In reality, he was suffering in his soul and his body; that terrible pain didn't let him live normally.

Then the man timidly added,

"I can't stand this anymore. Can you pray for me?"

"Do you want to accept Jesus as your Lord?"

He replied:

"You know, I've always laughed at that. But today, when you told me that God sent you to the sauna for me... I've never heard anything like this in my life. I never expected to hear about God in a sauna and so openly. No one in all my life has ever told me that God sent someone to me because He loves me, sees how I suffer, and wants to answer my needs. When you said that, I laughed at you in my mind, but deep inside, I started to cry. That's why I caught up with you and brought you to my car. I want you to pray for me here."

We began to pray. He accepted Jesus into his heart, and then God healed him. The horrible pain left him! Glory to God! We talked some more, and I also prayed for his family and blessed the rest of his life. If you only heard the amazing testimony of what God did in his life after that! But that's not the point. I want to direct your attention to something else. When I returned to my hotel room, I noticed a shift in my worship. I felt that everything I had done in obedience to His voice had released His lordship. It was worship to God. YES, worship is not just songs and prayers, but also obedience to His voice.

You may wonder, "How do you grow in the lordship of God?" The more you obey His voice, the more His lordship will be released in your life. His voice is found in His presence. Through it, He guides you. He leads you beside still waters so you can hear Him, and He can lead you to paths of righteousness for His name's sake.

Reflection:

Make a decision to learn to hear His voice. Sometimes, the voice of God begins with a thought that comes from within you, and with that thought comes a heartbeat or an impulse, and you realize that it is not just an ordinary thought. That thought will gently nudge you forward while also bringing you a sense of peace, and maybe you will start asking yourself, "Will I be able to do that? I've never done this before. Do I really have to take this leap of faith?"—or something similar. But that thought doesn't leave you. When such a thought comes with an impulse, and your heart starts beating, you realize that God is giving you the opportunity to do His will. However, He will not force, pressure, or control you. You have the freedom to choose at that moment.

You may ask, "How will I know it's Him speaking and not my thoughts?" By trial and error. If you follow what you hear and see success, it is Him. And if there is no result, it was your flesh or another influence. It's as simple as that. You need to learn to discern His voice and train yourself. Learning to discern His voice is a spiritual art; don't be afraid to try. That's how you'll learn to recognize His voice. I've made mistakes when I was learning, too, and not everything I heard and did was something God told me to do. I admitted that and kept seeking the authentic voice of God. You need to learn and train yourself.

Remember instances when God spoke to you from within. You obeyed His voice, saw His hand—and saw the impossible become possible. Write down those testimonies. They will remind you of God's presence and strengthen your faith.

_____

_____

_____

_____

_____

_____

_____

_____

_____

_____

Activation:

Spend the next 15 minutes praying in tongues and then another 15 minutes waiting in silence and stillness in His presence. Listen to His voice in the quiet of your secret place and wait to see what the Lord says, shows, or reveals inside your spirit. Record what you hear and see:

_____

_____

_____

_____

_____

_____

_____

_____

_____

_____

_____

His Guidance is in His Voice

Day 4

Psalm 92

A Psalm. A Song for the Sabbath day.

¹ *It is* good to give thanks to the Lord, and to sing praises to Your name, O Most High;

² To declare Your lovingkindness in the morning, and Your faithfulness every night,

³ On an instrument of ten strings, on the lute, and on the harp, with harmonious sound.

⁴ For You, Lord, have made me glad through Your work; I will triumph in the works of Your hands.

⁵ O Lord, how great are Your works! Your thoughts are very deep.

⁶ A senseless man does not know, nor does a fool understand this.

⁷ When the wicked spring up like grass, and when all the workers of iniquity flourish, *it is* that they may be destroyed forever.

⁸ But You, Lord, *are* on high forevermore.

⁹ For behold, Your enemies, O Lord, for behold, Your enemies shall perish; all the workers of iniquity shall be scattered.

¹⁰ But my horn You have exalted like a wild ox; I have been anointed with fresh oil.

¹¹ My eye also has seen *my desire* on my enemies; my ears hear *my desire* on the wicked who rise up against me.

¹² The righteous shall flourish like a palm tree, he shall grow like a cedar in Lebanon.

¹³ **Those who are planted in the house of the Lord shall flourish in the courts of our God.**

¹⁴ They shall still bear fruit in old age; they shall be fresh and flourishing,

¹⁵ To declare that the Lord is upright; *He is* my rock, and *there is* no unrighteousness in Him.

HAVE YOU EVER WONDERED WHAT *"planted in the house"* and *"flourish in the courts"* mean? (see Psalm 92:14). Prophetically, those who are planted in the house are those who have placed themselves in the presence of God. Notice: they do not visit His presence from time to time; they plant themselves there. They abide there, live, dwell, and do everything from His presence. And what is the result? Visible evidence and the fruit of the Spirit in their lives. You plant yourself in His presence, and everything in your life begins to flourish. You plant yourself in His house, and you thrive in the courts. When you plant yourself in the house, you prosper.

In verse 14, it goes on to say that these trees bear fruit and are vibrant and healthy, even as they age. It means that strength, freshness, and the ability to bear fruit do not depend on your age (whether you are young or old) but rather on the environment you place yourself in. A person who grows in intimacy with God and who has planted himself in His presence becomes firmly established in the eternal nature of God. Thus, he will be like a tree planted by streams of water whose leaf does not wither and who will bear fruit in due season; whatever he does shall prosper (see Psalm 1:3).

If you want to bear fruit in your life, don't focus on producing fruit. Focus on the foundation —God's presence: it must be the highest priority in your life. Why is His presence significant? Because His voice is in His presence. His leading is in His voice. And there will be success in obeying His leading; you will see fruit in your life.

I remember when we started outreach ministry in our church. We went to different areas of the city every Saturday, preached the gospel, and prayed for people on the streets. I was a youth pastor at that time. We understood that the Lord's commission is to go and preach the Good News to all people, so we began to do this with our youth. However, we spent much time and effort with no visible results. We went to do what God commanded in His Word, but there was no fruit. People reacted indifferently most of the time, and there were no testimonies of the glory of God. It really got under my skin.

One Saturday, while on the way to church, I was meditating and praying specifically about this, "God, what are we doing wrong? We dedicate so much time to this effort and do what You command us to do. You said we need to carry the Good News, and we do… but there is no fruit. Please teach me. How should outreach ministry be done? How do You see it? What are we doing wrong?" I was still praying about it when suddenly, I saw a large truck owned by the store "Target" switch lanes and start driving right in front of me. The back of the truck had a large image of the red target on a white background. I drove, looking straight at the target, and inside, I heard God's voice. The Holy Spirit told me, "My command to go to all the nations and bring the Good News is everyone's mission. It is everyone's calling, but if you incline yourself to hear My voice on this mission, you will hit right on target, and your labor will produce fruit." That's it! This was His answer to my prayer. At that moment, I realized that you should not run around in every direction and invest yourself in all possible trips and projects but be led by the Spirit of God in everything. "If you hear My voice and My guidance in this command to preach the gospel, I will direct your every step, and you will hit right on target every time," the Holy Spirit said again. I realized that I had been boxing blindfolded in our outreach ministry this whole time, thus missing the target.

So, I arrived at the church, where we gathered before going to the streets. I approached my friend Serge, who, by the way, is now one of our pastors in our Flame of Fire church. And I said to him, "Serge. When we split into groups, you are coming with me. I feel that God has shown me something. Today, we will do things differently." After the prayer, Serge and I drove to the park near the Capitol Building in downtown Sacramento, where there's always people sitting, resting, or walking around the park.

When we arrived, I explained, "Let's walk around and pray in the Spirit until we hear what God wants us to do." I don't remember exactly how long we walked and prayed; it was probably around 30 minutes or so. Suddenly, we both felt drawn to one person. It was a Hispanic man sitting alone under a tree. Still praying in the Spirit, Serge and I looked at him, then at each other. We both realized that God was directing us to him.

We approached this man and greeted him, and I said, "Hey, don't let this seem strange to you, but God brought us here and showed you to us so we could tell you about Jesus and pray with you." I didn't beat around the bush; I told him exactly why we were there. He lowered his head and began to cry. I tried to ask him what was wrong, but he interrupted me and said:

"I want you to hear my story. I'm from San Jose, California. Eight months ago, everything started to fall apart in my life. It was 2008 when the housing crisis hit. San Jose had a substantial market collapse. I had a good job at that time, and everything was good, too—I had a family, children, and a lovely house. I was making good money. My family wasn't in need. When this economic collapse happened, I was abruptly fired from my job. Over the next three months, all our savings ran out. I tried to find a job, but I couldn't. Soon, I couldn't pay for the house, and the bank repossessed it. We found ourselves on the street. Around the same time, my father was diagnosed with cancer. It was a tragedy for me. I was by his side and helped him as much as I could, but he died shortly after he was diagnosed. I started arranging my father's funeral. Aside from all of this, I still couldn't find a job. Life was so hard that my wife couldn't stand it. She left me, took our kids, and moved here to Sacramento. Can you imagine? In just a few months, I lost my job, house, father, wife, and children. They all left me. I've lost everything. I'm all alone."

"Two weeks ago, I attempted suicide by cutting my veins, and I still don't know who saved me! I only remember opening my eyes in the hospital. The first thing I said was, "Why? God, why did You let me live? I want to die. I have no purpose in life. Nobody needs me, and I am alone. Why do I need to live? If You are there, then why are You not answering me?"

"Shortly after, I was discharged from the hospital and contacted my wife. I wanted to see my children, so I'm here in Sacramento. My wife is bringing our children here at noon. I was waiting for them, looking at heaven and shouting inside, 'Why? God, why? Why did You let me live? What is the point of my life? If You are real, answer me. Who are You? What do I need to do?' And out of nowhere, you two appeared in front of me. You completely interrupted my thoughts, saying God sent you here to tell me about Jesus and pray for me."

As he was finishing his story, tears flowed down his face.

"What should I do? Tell me?" – he asked, sighing heavily.

"Let's start by genuinely accepting Jesus into your heart as your Lord and personal Savior."

We started praying, and he received Jesus. Then we prayed for his family, future, and destiny to be restored; we prayed for his children, too. We started talking to him, answering his questions, and encouraging him in faith. Soon, his children arrived. We exchanged phone numbers and parted.

A few weeks later, Serge contacted him and heard his testimony of what happened after our prayer—His family and relationships with his children were miraculously restored by God, giving him a newfound sense of purpose in life. Praise the Lord!

While driving home that day, the "Target" sign was still vividly in my mind, and I understood what it meant to hit the target. Success (bearing fruit for His glory) is connected to obedience to His voice, not just your efforts. His voice leads you and gives you an understanding of what to do, how to do it, and when to do it so you don't labor in vain but hit the target each time. Trust me, God wants to see this even more than you do.

The Holy Spirit wants to teach you from the tiniest steps that sometimes seem insignificant to us. The important thing is to learn to obey His voice in the small things, regardless of how big or small the task may be. For example, you might hear Him say, "Go do the dishes." It's not just about the dishes. A clean kitchen will probably make your spouse or parents happy. But the point is that you heard His voice and didn't ignore it. Why is this important? He trains your senses to know His voice. He teaches you to obey His voice and guidance using simple things.

I remember walking up to the car recently, and God said, "You haven't opened the door to your wife for a long time." I turn around abruptly, run to her, and open the car door for her. I barely made it. Opening the door wasn't the point. The point was to hear His voice and obey quickly – God was also testing my reaction to His voice. Some might say, "But it's not that important." They are waiting for God to tell them to do something big. He will tell you something big and great when you have learned to obey Him in small things. God teaches you from small steps. He teaches you to respond to His voice quickly. Why is your quick reaction to His voice this important? The Holy Spirit once answered me, "I am developing this reaction in you so that when I need you, you can hear Me even if you're sleeping. I want to be able to count on you when I need you. I know that if I tell Peter, he will not hear; if I tell Julie, she will not hear; if I tell the pastor, he will not hear, but when I tell you, you instantly react to My voice. I want to know that I have a man who will react quickly to My voice and do what I say."

Reflection:

Don't ignore even the minor things when you hear His voice in your spirit. He will begin teaching you using simple tasks: call that person, clean this, buy this, help with his, give this, tell this… You will feel His voice as an impulse, a tug in your spirit. Don't ignore those impulses. He is training you. He is preparing your senses and developing a quick reaction to His voice. Therefore, pay attention to the urges within you.

_____

_____

_____

_____

_____

_____

_____

Activation:

Spend the next 15 minutes praying in tongues and then another 15 minutes waiting in silence and stillness in His presence. Listen to His voice in the quiet of your secret place and wait to see what the Lord says, shows, or reveals inside your spirit. Record what you hear and see:

_____

_____

_____

_____

_____

Read Until the Word Speaks to You

Day 5

Psalm 1

¹ Blessed *is* the man who walks not in the counsel of the ungodly, nor stands in the path of sinners, nor sits in the seat of the scornful;

² But his delight is in the law of the Lord, and in His law he meditates day and night.

³ He shall be like a tree planted by the rivers of water, that brings forth its fruit in its season, whose leaf also shall not wither; and whatever he does shall prosper.

⁴ The ungodly *are* not so, but *are* like the chaff which the wind drives away.

⁵ Therefore the ungodly shall not stand in the judgment, nor sinners in the congregation of the righteous.

⁶ For the Lord knows the way of the righteous, but the way of the ungodly shall perish.

"How do you read the Bible?" —I am often asked this question.

I answer:

"I don't just read it; I live in it. I began to live in such a way that I would always dwell in the Word. I opened the Bible after I repented in 2002 and still haven't closed it."

"It seems to be the same verses of Scripture that we have read a hundred times, and you explain it entirely differently. We've never seen it that way before. How do you do it? How do you read and understand the Word?"

Let me answer:

"Read the letters until you fall into the Word!"

I often quote this phrase because I once heard it from God, "Read the letters until you fall into the Word, and the Word starts talking to you." I live by this principle.

It's important to understand that letters (written text) and the Word are different. Many people read the Bible. They know the Scriptures by heart and can even quote entire chapters from the Bible—but this is not enough. These are just letters, and they can't change you. The scribes and Pharisees also read the Scriptures and knew entire passages by heart, but that didn't change them. They did not know the Word, and the Word was not in them. Learning the letter doesn't change you; what has the power to transform you is God's Word. I will say more: the fact that you go to church and feel the presence of the Holy Spirit does not change you. What changes you is the Word. Someone might object, "Andrey, how can you say that? The presence of the Holy

Spirit definitely changes people." Allow me to explain. At the very beginning of creation, the earth was without form and void, and the Spirit of God hovered over the face of the waters (see Genesis 1:2). That means the presence of God was there, and so was chaos. And yet, at the same time, the earth was formless, and nothing changed until the Word of God was voiced from this presence! Likewise, people can feel the presence of the Holy Spirit in their lives, but their lives are a mess, and nothing changes. Why? Because the Holy Spirit works in partnership with the Word of God. You must have the Word in your life. The Word changes you! Not a letter, not a presence, but the living Word that comes from the mouth of God!

> *In the beginning was the Word, and the Word was with God, and the Word was God. He was in the beginning with God. All things were made through Him, and without Him nothing was made that was made* (John 1:1-4).

In the beginning, there was no Bible. In the beginning was the living Word; everything came into being through the Word. God began to create with His Word. His Words are spirit and life (see John 6:63). His wealth and wisdom are endless. The essence of His eternal nature is within His Word, inviting us to dive in.

What does it mean to read the letter until the Word speaks to you? How does this practically happen? I saw a vision while praying one day. A microwave oven appeared in front of me. The door opened, popcorn kernels were placed inside, the timer and the temperature were set, and the oven was turned on. I observed how everything inside began to spin and heat up, and at some point, the popcorn began to burst open.

And then the Holy Spirit explained, "Dry popcorn kernels are like the letters you read. The microwave represents your inner man. Your inner man should always be connected to My temperature so that every time you read and put the Scripture inside of you, it comes to life." I asked, "What's the key? How do we connect to Your temperature?" He said, "Through My presence and praying in the Spirit." The Holy Spirit is within you to give life to the letter you read. Therefore, if you want the Word to come alive and overtake you, always combine praying in the Spirit with reading the Scriptures. You need the presence of the Holy Spirit for the Word to come alive in your life. So, pray in the Spirit and dwell in the Scripture until the Scripture begins to "pop" inside you, come to life, and the Word starts speaking to you. The Word begins to correct, rebuke, guide, instruct, and encourage—it becomes a lamp to your feet. It speaks and begins to change you from within.

People often seek God's knowledge and revelation but don't fill themselves with the Scripture. That is a problem. Therefore, stay in the Scripture, read the letter, meditate, and pray in the Spirit to build yourself up. Do all this so the Holy Spirit can bring the Word to life within you.

In Psalm 1, it is written: *"But his delight is in the law of the Lord, and in His law he meditates day and night"* (Psalm 1:2). The truth is, it would be hard to meditate on the letter day and night, and you would forget what you read pretty quickly. But when the Word starts speaking to you, you can't help but think about it all the time; you will think about the revelation and constantly marvel at what God has revealed, what God has said, and what God has shown. You'll be captivated by His Word and start thinking about it day and night.

This is the meditation that Psalm 1:2 speaks of. And do you know what will happen next? You will become a tree planted by rivers of water, whose leaf shall not wither.

Today, I only wrote a little so you would start practicing these principles and immerse yourself in His Word.

Reflection:

Would you like God to reveal His Word to you? Having the Scripture inside you is essential so the Holy Spirit can give life to this Word.

1.   Don't randomly hop around the Bible. Read in order. Open Matthew and read sequentially through Revelation. When you have finished, go back to Matthew and read again until the end of Revelation. Meditate on the words of Jesus.

2.   Do not read in sections or by chapters. Read the books as one complete message: Matthew, Mark, Luke, and John. Do not extract chapters or verses out of the concept of the whole book. If you learn to read by the book, then you will learn to think by the book. I learned to consider not just the verses of Scripture but think in terms of the book, the whole message, and the entire concept embedded in each book. This is very important. So now, when the Holy Spirit reminds me of a verse in Scripture, I see the complete picture of what He wants to say.

3.   Don't worry about how many chapters you read in one sitting. Focus on the word speaking to you. How? Read in His presence

and ask the Holy Spirit to talk to you through His word. Pray that He will enlighten the eyes of your heart. Ask Him to reveal the Scriptures to you. This is of utmost importance.

4.   The goal is not to read through the whole Bible. The goal is for the Bible to come alive inside you, for the Word to start to speak to you, and for you to begin to think the Word. Read until the Scripture comes to life, until you feel that God has spoken to you, and until the depths of the Word have begun to open up to you.

_____

_____

_____

_____

_____

_____

_____

_____

_____

_____

_____

_____

_____

Activation:

Spend the next 15 minutes praying in tongues and then another 15 minutes waiting in silence and stillness in His presence. Listen to His voice in the quiet of your secret place and wait to see what the Lord says, shows, or reveals inside your spirit. Record what you hear and see:

_____

_____

_____

_____

_____

_____

_____

_____

_____

_____

_____

_____

_____

The Power of Praise

Day 6

Psalm 8

To the Chief Musician. On the instrument of Gath. A Psalm of David.

[1] O Lord, our Lord, how excellent *is* Your name in all the earth, Who have set Your glory above the heavens!

[2] Out of the mouth of babes and nursing infants You have ordained strength, because of Your enemies, that You may silence the enemy and the avenger.

[3] When I consider Your heavens, the work of Your fingers, the moon and the stars, which You have ordained,

[4] What is man that You are mindful of him, and the son of man that You visit him?

[5] For You have made him a little lower than the angels, and You have crowned him with glory and honor.

[6] You have made him to have dominion over the works of Your hands; You have put all *things* under his feet,

[7] All sheep and oxen—even the beasts of the field,

[8] The birds of the air, and the fish of the sea that pass through the paths of the seas.

[9] O Lord, our Lord, how excellent *is* Your name in all the earth!

I STARTED HAVING A BACK PROBLEM many years ago. I still don't know how it started. It could have been in my teenage years or a little later. Anyway, the point is that I just started having back pain whenever I sat still for long periods of time. In addition, I could not lower my head all the way—I had a pinched nerve somewhere, and when I did lower my head, it felt like needles were piercing into my neck and back. I went to the doctor, the chiropractor, and other specialists. They could not figure out the cause or provide relief. I wasn't overly bothered by this and was going about my life like usual. I just didn't put my head in painful positions and could manage to get out of any situation without explaining to everyone that I had back problems. But going to the barbershop was a different story. Whenever they cut my hair from the back, they asked me to put my head down. I was ashamed to admit that I couldn't lower my head without feeling pain. So, I would lower my head, and severe pain would shoot through my back; I endured it as much as I could, although I could not lower my chin all the way. Because of this, getting my hair cut was a problem, and it continued for a while.

When I started spending time with God in the secret place, I would sit a lot to read my Bible and be still before God, and the back pain would often start distracting me.

One evening in my old apartment, I knelt to worship God, and my back started to hurt again. The pain began to aggravate me as it prevented me from focusing on the Lord and spending time with Him. Holy jealousy began to overtake me. I hated that pain. At that moment, I decided that nothing would stop me from worshiping God—my praise would be even louder than the pain. Through this pain, I began to worship God loudly and praise Him despite the circumstances. I focused all my attention on Him and worshiped. For 40 minutes straight, I walked and praised God, declaring His glory and exalting His name. I didn't ask God to heal me. I want to note that at that moment, it arose from within me, "The voice of my praise will be stronger than the voice of my physical condition and pain." I decided to place all my attention on Him and none on my issue. Soon, I even forgot about the pain. I was in His presence and felt His glory all around me. At some point, I distinctly felt heat passing through my entire body. At that moment, I didn't recognize what had happened; I didn't realize that God healed me. I was captivated by His presence and started spending time in the Word.

So, a few days later, I went to get a haircut again. When the barber began cutting my hair from the back, I automatically lowered my head, suddenly realizing I had no pain. At that moment, I could touch my chest with my chin without experiencing any discomfort! In the barber's chair, I realized what had happened that evening when I decided to praise God instead of focusing on my pain. God completely healed me! Hallelujah!

Psalm 8:2 says: *"Out of the mouth of babes and nursing infants You have ordained strength, because of Your enemies, that You may silence the enemy and the avenger."* Please understand: the enemies mentioned in this passage of the Bible are not people but everything that stands against God's plan: every form of disease, sickness, addiction, fear, anxiety, discouragement, poverty, curse, and evil spirit that hinders you from your calling, success, closeness to God, health, etc. Enemies are all the things that are at enmity with God and His will. He wants to silence His enemies. This means that God wants to shut the mouth of every sickness, curse, stress, and fear in your life. If sickness is God's enemy, it's your enemy, too.

I do not know what challenges you are facing today and what fights you are fighting in this season of your life. Sickness can manifest in your body, and addiction, fear, doubts, circumstances, and situations may start screaming in your face. You cannot cope with them on your own, but here's a principle that will shut the mouths of these enemies.

First, refrain from focusing on or exalting the problem. By shifting your attention to God's greatness and proclaiming who He is, you're activating God's glory. Then, the Lord will come out of this praise and close the mouths of these enemies, situations, circumstances, poverty, and sicknesses. Learn to set your eyes on Jesus Christ and look at your life through Him. Even though negative thoughts and complaints might be your reality right now, know that vocalizing them gives access to the enemy. Instead of complaining and stressing about how difficult your life is, how tired you are, and how horrible and hopeless everything looks, shift your focus and start praising God for who He is. Your praises to God shut the mouths of your enemies. You should practice this not only in church but also in the car, in the kitchen, in the office, or while you're playing soccer on a field… always praise Him. Try to fall asleep with the words, "God, You are the Lord of my life. You are above all. You are Holy. You are greater than anything I can ever imagine…" and wake up with the words, "The LORD is my Shepherd; I will lack nothing. This is the day the Lord has made! I will rejoice and be glad in it!" This praise not only shuts the enemy's mouth but also releases God's power and strength into your life!

I was reminded of a story shared by Derek Prince in one of his sermons. One day, a woman brought her husband to his house for prayer. Her husband needed deliverance. When worship began, the man couldn't stand it. He began to get nauseous, shake, and squirm, and he ran to the door to leave the house. While he hurriedly put on his shoes, Derek Prince turned to him and said, "If you leave this atmosphere of worship, the enemy (demon) that torments you will remain in you. But if you make an effort to stay in this atmosphere, the demon will leave—that spirit won't be able to stand it, and it will come out of you." The man decided to stay, and God completely freed him in that atmosphere of praise and worship.

Start worshiping God in your life. Concentrate all your attention on Who He is. Revelation of Who God is will naturally give birth to praise, and you cannot remain silent. The greater your understanding and revelation of who God is, the greater the power of your praise will be. You will naturally praise God and proclaim His goodness!

Still don't know where to start? Your praise should be louder than your inner doubts and other voices. Don't whisper. Don't look at other people. Raise your voice and praise Him! Start declaring Who He is and expressing your love to Him. Start quoting Scriptures that declare His authority, lordship, and greatness. Just start worshiping Him:

> *"You are the LORD, My Shepherd! You are my refuge! You are my shield! You are my God, my Healer, my Deliverer. You are the truth and life. You are the bread that came down from heaven. You are the LORD of my life!"*

And then, when all your attention is on Him, let your entire being glorify Him.

God created my feet, so I'll praise the Lord with my feet. God made my hands, so I'll praise the Lord with my hands. God formed my eyes, so I will keep my eyes on His greatness. I'll worship Him with my whole being.

Many believers never realized why David danced. Dance is an art and an instrument of praise and worship. Dance is a strong expression of authority and power. It is written: *"Behold, I give you the authority to trample on serpents and scorpions, and over all the power of the enemy, and nothing shall by any means hurt you"* (see Luke 10:19). Keep in mind that when we worship God with dancing, we prophetically trample on the enemy and affirm the authority of the Lord, because He put all the enemies under His feet. My dance is my praise, directed at the One who is My Lord, Savior, Deliverer, and Healer. Only He is worthy of all the praise. Therefore, I will not stop dancing. I strongly refuse to say that dancing is a worldly practice.

People often stick to their beliefs, even if it means living in a dry atmosphere filled with human regulations, oppression, and negativity. But guess what? If we break free from the opinions of others, removing all timidity, pride, fear, and vanity, we make every crooked path straight and pave the way for the Lord and His glory to come.

Dancing, flagging, and clapping are not just emotional expressions. They flow from a revelation of who God is. It's not just my feelings that are involved; it's my faith. Let me clarify: I'm not saying people should jump, dance, and clap just to do it. I want to say, don't limit your expressions of praise to a few limited sets of actions just because it's what you've been taught. Don't think people can't praise God any other way than what you grew up with. Just because you were taught to praise God a certain way doesn't mean it's the only way to praise Him. Look what the Scripture says:

> *Praise Him with the sound of the trumpet; praise Him with the lute and harp!*
>
> *Praise Him with the timbrel and dance; praise Him with stringed instruments and flutes!*
>
> *Praise Him with loud cymbals; praise Him with clashing cymbals!*
>
> *Let everything that has breath praise the Lord. Praise the Lord!* (Psalm 150:3-6).

Some people have trumpets and organs in their churches. Hallelujah! Don't judge them; let them praise God from their hearts. Do not condemn someone who praises God differently than you. Let the trumpets, drums, harps, strings, and every other instrument praise the Lord. The instruments we use and the forms of expression are not the main point. If you breathe, use everything, and I mean everything that God created to praise Him. It is written: *"Let everything that has breath praise the Lord!"* Praise Him! May His house be filled with glory!

I recently stopped by Starbucks to grab some coffee and ran into some familiar faces—a group of young men with a guitar. Curiosity got the best of me, so I asked them, "What's the guitar for?" They answered in unison, "We're worshiping the Lord here." I thought, "My God, no one can stop what the Spirit of the Lord is reviving and restoring all over the face of the earth." As someone who travels to different nations, I see this everywhere I go: young people are coming together just to worship God. No one asks them to, no one forces them, and no one can stop them from getting together to worship God. People might oppose them and try to prevent them from gathering, but they can't. This movement of worship starts spreading even further: they gather in houses, in cafes, on the streets, in parks, in town squares, everywhere. This praise is connected to the revelation of Who God is! His praise will go on and on throughout all the earth, and all the earth will be filled with the knowledge of the glory of the Lord (see Habakkuk 2:14). Hallelujah!

Reflection:

What are you fighting for in this season of your life? What things in your life oppose God's will? (Remember, these are not people or organizations). Determine who your enemy is. Write this down and decide that the voice of your praise will be louder than the voice of your enemy. I'm confident that you will experience a significant victory in this area in time.

_____

_____

_____

_____

Activation:

Spend the next 15 minutes praying in tongues and then another 15 minutes waiting in silence and stillness in His presence. Listen to His voice in the quiet of your secret place and wait to see what the Lord says, shows, or reveals inside your spirit. Record what you hear and see:

_____

_____

_____

_____

_____

_____

_____

_____

_____

_____

_____

_____

_____

Arm Yourself!

Day 7

Ephesians 6:10-17

[10] Finally, my brethren, be strong in the Lord and in the power of His might.

[11] Put on the whole armor of God, that you may be able to stand against the wiles of the devil.

[12] For we do not wrestle against flesh and blood, but against principalities, against powers, against the rulers of the darkness of this age, against spiritual hosts of wickedness in the heavenly places.

[13] Therefore take up the whole armor of God, that you may be able to withstand in the evil day, and having done all, to stand.

[14] Stand therefore, having girded your waist with truth, having put on the breastplate of righteousness,

[15] and having shod your feet with the preparation of the gospel of peace;

[16] above all, taking the shield of faith with which you will be able to quench all the fiery darts of the wicked one.

[17] And take the helmet of salvation, and the sword of the Spirit, which is the word of God.

A S I MENTIONED EARLIER, PSALM 91 shows us what God's lordship looks like in our lives. I want to direct your attention to the final verses of this Psalm, where God says the following: *"... because he has known My name."* In other words, the Lord says, "I will cover him with all My promises and goodness because he has known My name!" *What name? The LORD.* This is key! Just think about it: knowing Him as LORD releases His lordship and moves God to act on your behalf, and He does so for Himself and His name.

Let's look at the New Testament. In Ephesians 6:10, the apostle Paul urges: *"Finally, my brethren, **be strong in the Lord** and in the power of His might."* How can you be strong in the Lord? Knowing His name provides the foundation for your life. The more you come to know Him as Lord, the more His lordship will strengthen you, and the more His power will be released through you. Let me repeat: obeying God will lead you to know Him as LORD, and when you know His name, His lordship and power is released. So, both Psalm 91 and Ephesians 6 emphasize the lordship of God and direct our attention to get to know Him as LORD.

"Finally, my brethren, be strong in the Lord and in the power of His might"—this is the main point! Everything that Paul writes next is connected to this phrase. The verses that follow explain how to be strong in the Lord. So, let's dive in.

"Put on the whole armor of God." Some believers attempt to apply this Scripture literally. They imagine the armor of God as an invisible set of armor they wear and declare, "I put on the breastplate of righteousness, I put on the helmet of salvation, I take the shield of faith…"

But this description is symbolic, not literal. This is not a proclamation. We must look deeper to see what the apostle Paul is talking about.

You don't put on the whole armor of God by declaring it every morning and then believing that you walk in this armor. The apostle Paul calls us to put on the knowledge of the Lord Himself and who we are in Him:

1. *Stand therefore, girding your waist with truth*—this is your position in Christ Jesus. He is the truth, and you position yourself in Him. In other words, you must stand like a son in His righteousness, power, and destiny. In Christ Jesus, you are justified, redeemed, and restored. God is for you, not against you. This is your position. Gird yourself with the truth that He is your Father, and you are His son. Stand firm on this truth. Gird your waist with it.

2. *Having put on the breastplate of righteousness.* It means to be clothed in the righteousness of Jesus. And every time an enemy (whether it be demons, sickness, or circumstances) comes to attack you, the first thing they have to get through is what you're clothed in spiritually. And because you are clothed in Jesus, nothing will hurt you. The breastplate of righteousness is the revelation of who Jesus is and who you are in Him. And the more profound your revelation, the thicker this armor becomes. This armor now protects you, not because you declare every morning that you put on the breastplate of righteousness, but because you have known His name.

3. *And having shod your feet with the preparation of the gospel of peace.* This speaks of living out our purpose. When we stand in the truth and wear the breastplate of righteousness, we are protected,

so we can focus on fulfilling our destinies as children of God. Regardless of our circumstances or current season, we should always be ready to preach the gospel. We are His messengers, His voice, and His ambassadors. Sharing the gospel should become our way of life. Note that I'm not talking about occasionally going on a mission trip. We put this readiness on our feet so we can preach the good news whenever the opportunity arises. This readiness becomes our weapon, enabling us to destroy the kingdom of darkness and expand the territory of the Kingdom of God.

4. *Above all, taking the shield of faith with which you will be able to quench all the fiery darts of the wicked one.* His faith starts operating in you. This is the next level of knowing God and growing in Him.

Every piece of the armor is interconnected; the shield repels the attacks, and the helmet protects your head.

5. *And take the helmet of salvation.* The helmet of salvation is all about renewing your mind. When your mind is renewed, it becomes good soil for God's faith. The fiery darts of the wicked one are thoughts launched into your heart and mind. They are lies in the form of thoughts and ideas that attack our thinking. Therefore, the shield of faith and the helmet of salvation operate together — they do not allow these lies to be planted in your mind and heart. Again, through the knowledge of God and a renewed mindset, you are protected, and the fiery darts cannot harm you.

6. *And the sword of the Spirit, also known as the Word of God,* is a powerful weapon of authority. That is why the Word must abide in you, rooted in your thinking (not the letter, the Word). When the living Word is in your mouth, it becomes a mighty sword that

inflicts one defeat after another on the enemy. Let me emphasize again that it will be easy for the devil to deceive you when the Word isn't in you. But when His Word is in you, you can take the Word of God as a sword and confront the enemy with the authority of Christ.

So, each element of the armor of God is associated with a particular area of knowledge and understanding:

Standing with your waist girded with truth is all about your position in Christ Jesus and your restored sonship.

The breastplate of righteousness is the knowledge of His righteousness in you and you being clothed in Jesus.

The preparation of the gospel of peace on your feet is a readiness to preach the gospel at all times and thereby destroy the kingdom of darkness.

The shield of faith is God's divine faith in you that comes through abiding in Him.

The helmet of salvation safeguards your mind, not allowing the arrows of the evil one to pierce through.

The sword of the Spirit is the living Word of God given to you to confront and defeat the adversary.

As you can see, the whole armor of God has more to do with knowing the Lord than proclamation. There was a season when God taught me this valuable lesson.

I remember one night when a phone call woke me up. It was about one o'clock in the morning. A family from our church called me and started pleading with me, "Pastor Andrey, please come and pray for our daughter. She's having demonic manifestations." I was a youth pastor at the time.

They were frightened. I tried to figure out the root of the manifestation and how everything unfolded. The parents weren't sure what their daughter got into; they only knew she had become very fond of Metallica, a demonic band, and other dark related things. The girl was manifesting disturbing behavior, and her God-fearing Christian parents were helpless. I reassured them, "Don't fret. I'll call the pastor and a few brothers, and we will all come together."

I tried calling our pastor and other leaders, but no one answered their phones. It was the middle of the night, and they were all sound asleep. I thought, "What should I do?" Suddenly, Ephesians 6 came to my mind. I started reciting this passage in my memory and felt the presence of God over me, and Him saying, "You're protected. You have nothing to fear. Your weapon is the Word of God; it's not the pastor or your friends. I am with you and have given you the power and authority to trample—go forth and minister."

So, I decided to go there by myself. The family lived nearby, so getting to their house didn't take long. As I approached the door, the Holy Spirit said, "Walk in the house as a son of God. That is who you are. Don't let fear or caution guide you; walk in boldly, armed with truth. You are My ambassador, endowed with the power to trample on all the enemy's power, and nothing by any means shall harm you. My Word is a sword in your mouth—strike the enemy with it."

I went inside the house. Not the most pleasant sight. This girl was on the floor on all fours. When she heard my footsteps, she raised her head and stared at me. The demonic spirit within her started growling:

"Why did you come? What do you want from me?"

I knew it wasn't her speaking. The demon in her immediately recognized who walked in.

"I came to proclaim God's Word over her and cast you out! You no longer have power, and you will leave her now."

I stepped toward her, but she unexpectedly jumped at me and swiftly changed direction, snatching my Bible out of my hands.

And then, I've never seen anything like this in my life: She opened my Bible and quickly started flipping through the pages—flipping flipping flipping… as if she was on a quest searching for something—and then, to my surprise, she tore out a page. The demon's audacity caught me completely off guard. I quickly retrieved my Bible from her hands, but she still managed to tear that one page out and toss it on the floor. I began to proclaim the Word of God over her and command all unclean spirits to get out. To summarize, the girl received deliverance that night. After that, I took my Bible and thought, "What did she tear out?" When I picked up that piece of paper, it was Ephesians 6. The demon in her found that specific chapter and tore it out from my Bible with such speed that I can't even explain. It was unreal.

When I returned home, I couldn't help but think about what happened, "There must be something in this chapter that I don't know, don't understand yet, something that satan is afraid of and therefore attacking." I began to dig deeper into the Epistle to the Ephesians. Studying that book was a profound season in my life. I wanted to understand the overall concept of the book of Ephesians. So, I want you to remember the key phrase in that book: *"Finally, my brethren, be strong in the Lord and in the power of His might."*

That is why being in His presence and having a personal relationship with the Lord is crucial. His power is activated in the areas of your life where you have knowledge and revelation of Him.

When I embrace my identity as a child of God, His power works through me.

When I wear the breastplate of righteousness, His power works through me.

When I am ready to preach the gospel of peace, His power works through me.

When I walk in faith, His power works through me.

When I wear the helmet of salvation, I am protected by the power of His might.

When I speak God's word, His power works through me.

Reflection:

Take a moment to jot down and memorize Ephesians 6:10-17. Focus on the main concept, "Be strengthened in the Lord and in the power of His might."

_____

_____

_____

_____

_____

_____

_____

Activation:

Spend the next 15 minutes praying in tongues and then another 15 minutes waiting in silence and stillness, basking in His presence. Listen to His voice in the quiet of your secret place and wait to see what the Lord says, shows, or reveals inside your spirit. Record what you hear and see:

_____

_____

_____

_____

_____

_____

_____

_____

_____

_____

_____

The Seven Spirits of God

Day 8

Isaiah 61:1-4

[1] "The Spirit of the LORD God is upon Me, because the LORD has anointed Me to preach good tidings to the poor; He has sent Me to heal the brokenhearted, to proclaim liberty to the captives, and the opening of the prison to *those who are* bound;

[2] To proclaim the acceptable year of the LORD, and the day of vengeance of our God; to comfort all who mourn,

[3] To console those who mourn in Zion, to give them beauty for ashes, the oil of joy for mourning, the garment of praise for the spirit of heaviness; that they may be called trees of righteousness, the planting of the LORD, that He may be glorified."

[4] And they shall rebuild the old ruins, they shall raise up the former desolations, and they shall repair the ruined cities, the desolations of many generations.

Isaiah 11:2-3

[2] The Spirit of the LORD shall rest upon Him, the Spirit of wisdom and understanding, the Spirit of counsel and might, the Spirit of knowledge and of the fear of the LORD.

[3] His delight is in the fear of the LORD, and He shall not judge by the sight of His eyes, nor decide by the hearing of His ears…

LET'S DISCOVER HOW GOD REIGNS from His throne, thinking and ruling over His creation. Revelation 4:5 says: *"And from the throne proceeded lightnings, thunderings, and voices. Seven lamps of fire were burning before the throne, which are the seven Spirits of God."* A lamp of fire gives light and illuminates everything around it. Seven lamps of fire are burning before the Lord's throne—these are the seven spirits of God: the spirit of wisdom and understanding, the spirit of counsel and might, the spirit of knowledge and godliness, and the fear of the Lord (reverential and obedient fear of the Lord (see Isaiah 11:2 AMP)). The seven spirits of God represent His mindset and the way He operates.

When Isaiah prophesied the coming of the Messiah to this earth, he said that the Spirit of the LORD and the seven spirits of God would rest upon Him! In other words, Isaiah foresaw that Jesus would be under the complete lordship of God and think like Him:

> *The Spirit of the LORD shall rest upon Him, the Spirit of wisdom and understanding, the Spirit of counsel and might, the Spirit of knowledge and of the fear of the Lord. His delight is in the fear of the Lord, and He shall not judge by the sight of His eyes, nor decide by the hearing of His ears* (Isaiah 11:2-3).

These are the seven spirits of God who give divine light and understanding, counsel and might, wisdom and knowledge, and the fear of the Lord—when they rest upon you, you don't judge by what your eyes see, nor decide by what your ears hear; you adopt His perspective. It is essential to note that the seven spirits of God will operate in your life when you submit to God's lordship over you. They don't work outside of His lordship—they function only when the Spirit of the LORD is upon you. This circles us back to the topic of God's lordship.

I often proclaim this passage of Scripture over my life; perhaps many of you have heard me do so. When these rest upon you, you begin to see differently because physical things no longer influence your decisions. The testimony of others is no longer needed to discern what lies within someone's heart. This divine enlightenment comes from the Spirit of the LORD. This is how Jesus operated on earth. It must become our standard, and we should be passionate about following His way and example. The Bible says that we should have the mind of Christ and be constantly renewed in the spirit of our minds so that we may discern the will of God.

When the Spirit of the LORD is upon you, you receive divine understanding and knowledge. This happens to me often, especially as I'm preaching. As I surrender myself to the leading of the Holy Spirit, I begin to get revelations from within that are not in my notes. A thought comes that reveals God's wisdom. At that moment, the spirit of wisdom and understanding is operating, and I start to speak from the realm of the spirit.

When the Spirit of the LORD is upon you, your perception goes beyond the limitations of the human mind. Your spiritual eyes open, and you begin to see beyond what you see with your physical eyes. Divine counsel and guidance flow through you. When you align your thoughts and actions with God's way, you allow the Holy Spirit to do His work and glorify Jesus. I have experienced this numerous times in my life.

I was ministering in different cities all over Ukraine once. It was a whole tour. The last service was scheduled in Donetsk on a Saturday with one of the Messianic congregations. We drove to Donetsk early in the morning, and on the way to our destination, we decided to stop at a German gas station renowned for its delicious breakfasts.

So, we went there and ordered steaks with scrambled eggs for breakfast. While preparing the order, we grabbed some coffee and sat down. As we did, a bunch of young guys walked in, and they looked exactly like a stereotypical 90's gang. There were about 12 of them; all the guys were big and bulky. Among them was a young man who had once been a believer but returned to the world. One of our pastors recognized him.

These guys had been partying all night and were returning from some club or hang-out. They were loud and messy, and you could tell they already had been in a fight. They genuinely looked like they came to that gas station straight from the 90's.

Soon, we discovered that the one who walked away from God had his birthday that day. That's why these guys stopped by the gas station for a little morning celebration. They ordered some champagne and salted nuts; apparently, they had no money. This gang sat down next to us and started sharing the nuts and drinking the champagne. It was pretty evident that they were tired but still quite aggressive and ready to knock someone out.

We were just minding our business and sitting next to them. However, they began to tease and insult us. It was impossible to ignore their open and unapologetic rudeness. It felt like they were mocking us on behalf of the devil himself.

The pastor, who knew one of the guys, decided to have a heart-to-heart conversation with him. But he began by blaming this young man for walking away from God, comparing him to a dog returning to its vomit. I looked around, and I saw these guys fuming. The atmosphere became extremely tense in a matter of seconds.

The pastor insistently lectured this guy and then went outside, leaving us with this angry group of guys. And because he was part of our group, we were held responsible for his words. At some point, we overheard them mentioning they were about to start fighting. These guys were ready to beat us up. Despite their verbal attacks, we remained silent, staring at our coffee mugs and waiting for the steaks. Although, we very well understood that we were in trouble, and without a fight, we wouldn't be able to leave. But we were on our way to a church service.

We were outnumbered; there were a dozen of them and only a few of us. I buried my head in my hands and leaned over the table, "God, what should we do? This rough situation came out of nowhere. They're going to start fighting, and they will 100% beat us because you can see how jacked they are and that they do this all the time. It genuinely feels like we were set up..." I raised my head and saw the pastor walking determinately towards that guy again, ready to unleash round two with a new speech. I thought, "Oh, no! That's it; the show is about to begin." At that exact moment, I saw the waitress walking towards us, bringing a big platter with steaks and eggs. Suddenly, a thought struck me, and I clearly understood what needed to be done, "Right now, take these steaks and treat these guys. It's that guy's birthday."

It all happened simultaneously. The pastor approached that guy, and the waitress brought the steaks. Without wasting a second, I intercepted the tray with the steaks and eggs, and before the pastor had a chance to open his mouth, I said, "Guys, you're celebrating his birthday today. Let us treat all of you to a meal. Unfortunately, we are in a hurry to attend a church service now—we don't have any more time to eat. We just want to bless you. Can we gift you these steaks and wish you a happy birthday?"

They all stood up abruptly. All of them paused... Then, the atmosphere shifted. Despite their previous hostility and verbal aggression toward us, they now appeared confused and uncertain because we responded to their insults with kindness. Such a thing had never happened to them. They said:

"Well, yeah. Thank you, sure."

We gave them our steaks:

"Happy birthday! Blessings to you, guys."

And I quietly whispered to my friends:

"Brothers, time to leave. Breakfast is over. Let's get out of here while we still can!"

As we walked to the door, they kept standing there with the trays in their hands. At that moment, I felt there was an epiphany in the atmosphere. God revealed His wisdom, counsel, and strength, changing the situation. It was powerful!

We got on the bus and let out a sigh of relief. Then the pastor commented:

"Man, I wanted to tell him off again, but I didn't have time."

Silence ensued. We looked at each other and then asked him:

"You've got to be joking. Do you not understand that they wanted to beat us up?"

But God did not allow it. That situation showed me how the spirit of council works and how God manifests His power through it. We wouldn't have gotten out of that situation without a fight if we had tried to solve everything with our human minds. There would have been one option left: they would fight us, and we would have had to come to the service to preach the gospel all beaten up.

But God didn't let that happen. They watched us walk out with the trays still in their hands. Do you know why? When the Spirit of God gives you counsel, and when you're obedient to His lordship, His might and power manifest, and an epiphany occurs. Those guys rose to their feet before the greatness of God without even realizing it.

When your life is under His lordship, the mind of Christ begins to operate in you. He gives you an understanding of what to do, how, and when to do it. And you stand in awe of His might and greatness. This realization makes you tremble in awe of who God is. Take time to reflect on this truth and receive it into your life.

One day, God told me, "If you'll be zealous for this and completely surrender to My lordship, you will be empowered to walk on earth just like Jesus did. You will be able to perceive what others don't and to discern the times, seasons, My desires, and My will..." I don't know about you, but the thought of this excites me!

Reflection:

Do not beg in prayer, "God, please give me this," He has already sent His Spirit to this earth. Begin to receive, embrace it, and declare His lordship over your life with your mouth:

I receive the Spirit of the LORD, the spirit of wisdom and understanding, the spirit of counsel and might, the spirit of knowledge and godliness, and the fear of the Lord. I will not judge by what my eyes see or decide matters by what my ears hear.

The Spirit of the LORD God is upon Me, for the Lord has anointed Me to preach the good news to the poor, has sent Me to heal the broken-hearted, to proclaim liberty to the captives and open the prison doors to those who are bound, to proclaim the acceptable year of the Lord and the day of vengeance of our God; to comfort all those who mourn, to console those who mourn in Zion, that they will be given beauty instead of ashes, the oil of joy instead of mourning, the garment of praise instead of the spirit of heaviness. They will be called trees of righteousness, the planting of the Lord for His glory.

Holy Spirit, I'm yours. Lead me into all truth. Teach me to draw near to You with a pure heart. Take over my whole life. I receive Your lordship.

Proclaim this often. Declare His lordship over your life, and you will see how this will manifest in your life.

Activation:

Spend the next 15 minutes praying in tongues and then another 15 minutes waiting in silence and stillness in His presence. Listen to His voice in the quiet of your secret place and wait to see what the Lord says, shows, or reveals inside your spirit. Record what you hear and see:

_____

_____

_____

_____

_____

_____

_____

_____

_____

_____

_____

_____

_____

_____

_____

Fight for Hunger

Day 9

Psalm 63

A Psalm of David when he was in the wilderness of Judah.

¹ O God, You *are* my God; early will I seek You; my soul thirsts for You; my flesh longs for You in a dry and thirsty land where there is no water.

² So I have looked for You in the sanctuary, to see Your power and Your glory.

³ Because Your lovingkindness *is* better than life, my lips shall praise You.

⁴ Thus I will bless You while I live; I will lift up my hands in Your name.

⁵ My soul shall be satisfied as with marrow and fatness, and my mouth shall praise You with joyful lips.

⁶ When I remember You on my bed, I meditate on You in the *night* watches.

⁷ Because You have been my help, therefore in the shadow of Your wings I will rejoice.

⁸ My soul follows close behind You; Your right hand upholds me.

⁹ But those *who* seek my life, to destroy *it*, shall go into the lower parts of the earth.

¹⁰ They shall fall by the sword; they shall be a portion for jackals.

¹¹ But the king shall rejoice in God; everyone who swears by Him shall glory; but the mouth of those who speak lies shall be stopped.

E VER SINCE I REPENTED, I'VE made a consistent decision to seek God and do everything I can to get to know Him personally rather than live in superficial Christianity. I devoted my whole life to growing in God and obeying His voice so He could lead me to my destiny. I never thought it would be so difficult to keep my passion and stay on fire for Him. When people are born from above, they seek God passionately because they are hungry for Him. No one forces or pushes them. They want to pray, read the Word, and attend every church service because they don't want to do anything else. And so, their relationship with God starts to grow because of their hunger. Many people call it first love.

At first, spiritual hunger drives you, but you need more than just hunger to go further in God. You need to work on discipline. Then, as you develop discipline, you must fight to keep your hunger. I say this from experience; you must keep both discipline and hunger. There are very responsible and disciplined people who attend every service, serve in different areas of the church, pray, and study God's Word. But the hunger for God isn't there anymore, only their iron-willed discipline, which gives other people the impression that they are "spiritual Christians." That is why when you have developed discipline, do not stop. Continue to fight for spiritual hunger.

But how to do it?

In Psalm 63, David says,

> O God, you are my God; earnestly I seek You; my soul
> thirsts for You; my flesh faints for You, as in a dry and
> weary land where there is no water. So I have looked

> *upon you in the sanctuary, beholding your power and*
> *glory* (Psalm 63:1-2 ESV).

I started to meditate on that Psalm once, thinking, "David, what pushes you to seek God in the early hours of the morning? Where does this desire come from? Where does this discipline come from? What kind of passion is stronger than your desire for sleep? What is this force that empowers you to overcome your flesh and pushes you to discipline yourself?" This driving force is a deep hunger for God.

Further in the same Psalm, David writes:

> *... when I remember You upon my bed, and meditate*
> *on You in the watches of the night* (Psalm 63:6 ESV).

Wait, what? Where does he meditate on God? David thinks about Him in his bed, not during prayer or church service. God was on his mind even after praying.

I know what it's like to wake up and say, "Jesus, I love You. I cannot say it enough: I love You!"

I know what it's like to be unable to sleep because you're thinking about His greatness and glory.

I know what it's like not being able to sleep because you are meditating on the Word and His revelations.

I know what it's like to not sleep for days because your spirit is praying and interceding, and you don't want to stop it.

I know what it's like to wake up with a song of praise in your heart.

I also know what it's like not wanting to get up in the morning because the first thing you think about is where to get the money to pay your bills. I know what it's like not being able to sleep because you're drowning in trouble, fear, and stress.

David says, "I remember You upon my bed…" Why? His soul was thirsty, not because of his problems but because it yearned for God!

How do you determine whether you are hungry for God? Just check where your thoughts are when you fall asleep and when you get up. Is He on your mind? Answer these questions honestly, and you will understand whether or not you are hungry for God. If you read the Bible and pray but don't think about Him apart from those moments, you have built discipline but have lost your hunger.

Have you ever wondered why David was so hungry for God? Where did this passion and hunger come from? The ninth verse (ESV) gives us the answer: *"… my soul clings to you."* That's it! David's soul clung to God.

Has your soul clung to God? I often ask myself this question and test my own heart. How can you measure this? Once, the Holy Spirit used my relationship with my wife to explain this to me. At some point, my soul clung to her. Natasha was still my fiancée when my soul first clung to her. Do you know what started to happen? I longed for conversations with her, sought out every possible way to meet, and wanted to see and spend time with her. This hunger and thirst could not be explained or stopped.

I would wake up thinking about her, come home, and fall asleep thinking about her, too. I was ready to get up early and go to bed late just so we could talk more. I was awake deep into the night because my soul clung to her. This condition made me sleep-deprived and malnourished. It wasn't insomnia. I was up in the night watches because my soul clung to her. When I first saw Natasha, we had just met and were sitting at a table, and I was only looking after her; I noticed even the most minor details. All my attention was on her. This desire prompted me to take actions I would not have otherwise taken if my soul didn't cling to her. I wouldn't gift so many flowers, open so many doors, buy so many gifts, or behave like I did for anyone else. This passion fueled my soul, lifted me, and brought me to do great exploits. In short, pedal to the metal; there's no time to settle.

So, my usual behavior and actions have changed. I began to change for her sake just because I fell in love. Sometimes, it's difficult for us to change ourselves, but when our souls cling to God, we cannot help but change for His sake. I realized that no matter how much we try to change ourselves in some areas, we cannot. We need to seek God; we need Him, and when we cling to Him, that changes us. Thus, our soul must cling to the Lord—His love changes us.

Day after day, I check myself: How often do I think about Him? Is He in my thoughts? Do I fall asleep thinking about His word? Am I clinging to Him as much as I was 20 years ago?

That's all great, but what do you do if you lose your hunger? How do you get it back?

The answer is in Revelation 2:4-5 that says: *"Nevertheless I have this against you, that you have left your first love. Remember therefore from where you have fallen; repent and do the first works..."*

God once told me, "Remember what you did for your fiancée. Remember every little thing your passion pushed you to do. Remember and start doing those things for her again."

The first thing is to remember! Remember all the little things you did for Him: how you sought Him when you had first love, how you ran to the secret place, were captivated by Jesus, prayed, told people about God, and looked for every opportunity to serve others. You did these things because you were hungry for God, and your soul clung to Him. If you lost your first love, it's not because God took it away. It's because you didn't cultivate it further and allowed other things to satisfy your hunger.

Second: repent. It's that simple.

Third: return to your first works. Note that God did not say, "Return to your first love," He said, "Return to your first works." The question is not so much what you are doing for Him now as it is whether you are doing your first works. In your first love, you did things because you wanted, not because you had to, because of Him, not just for Him. There is a difference. God calls us to return to these first works that we did because of our hunger for Him. The first love did not fade away on its own; you abandoned it. Remember this peculiar state of first love. Recall the things you did for His sake and start doing them again. That will bring back your hunger and revive your first love!

If you left your first love:

1. Remember your first love. Remember every detail and be honest with yourself.

2. Repent. Admit that you don't have it anymore, and repent.

3. Return to the first works—start doing the things you used to do for His sake—it will reawaken your hunger and first love.

Friend, work on discipline, and fight for your hunger for God. Hunger will always lead you to see His power and glory. When you really want something, you will find an opportunity to get it. When you don't like something, you'll find a thousand excuses not to. I know that spiritually hungry people will go deeper and further in God. They will not be stuck in the same place; they will go from glory to glory!

Reflection:

Let's pause in this state and allow the Holy Spirit to test our hearts and speak to us.

_____

_____

_____

_____

_____

_____

_____

Activation:

Spend the next 15 minutes praying in tongues and then another 15 minutes waiting in silence and stillness in His presence. Listen to His voice in the quiet of your secret place and eagerly anticipate what the Lord says, shows, or reveals inside your spirit. Record what you hear and see:

_____

_____

_____

_____

_____

_____

_____

_____

_____

_____

_____

_____

_____

_____

_____

_____

_____

_____

_____

_____

_____

Father's Will

Day 10

Luke 5:15-16

[15] However, the report went around concerning Him all the more; and great multitudes came together to hear, and to be healed by Him of their infirmities.

[16] So He Himself often withdrew into the wilderness and prayed.

PLEASE REMEMBER THIS PASSAGE OF Scripture in Luke 5:15–16; it is essential. I am confident that as soon as you start putting into practice all I have shared in this journal and the book *"Not of this World,"* you will see a transformation in your life. The fruit of your close relationship with God will manifest and be evident. You will be amazed at how spiritual boldness, faith, and vision will come and grow in your life. God will begin to heal people through you, deliver them, and give you wisdom and the ability to see further and do His will.

You will notice that your hunger and close walk with God will begin to infect others, change the atmosphere, bring the fragrance of heaven, and give others life and hope. You will offer advice, and things will work out for good. You will pray and see heaven back you up. People will come to you and testify that your life has impacted them and that your hunger has infected them. Suddenly, testimonies and talk about God being with you will begin to spread. Your ministry will start to gain momentum. Success will come, and in that moment, it is vital that this fame does not get ahead of you so that you do not turn your attention from the Lord to your success.

As we come to the final chapter of this journal, I want to appeal to everyone who has started practicing the lessons and seeing the results. Keep going; you will see even more. Perhaps you will fully understand this final lesson only later, but even so, I strongly advise you to set aside at least one day every month and dedicate it entirely to the Lord. At least one day, but do it every single month. Make arrangements. Go and plan it right now; put this day in your calendar as the most important day of the month.

Next, find a place outside of your city to retreat with God. Why not in your house and not in your city? You need to disconnect yourself from everything you're attached to: your home, family, work, business, responsibilities, errands, and the community. In your city or town, you would feel like you're still in the system and connected to everyone and everything. Psychologically, it influences you. You must reach a condition where you subconsciously acknowledge, "I'm not home, and I'm not in town right now." And you can even answer people, "Sorry, I'm not in town..." There, you would be able to disconnect yourself emotionally, mentally, and psychologically. Then, you can stop time and be in the moment with God.

Start with one day each month, then extend this to a two or three-day retreat with the Lord. I inspire you to stretch your inner man with this practice of having retreats with God on a monthly basis. Learn to stop all ministry and serving and go to deserted places for one thing—to focus on your Father and His will. Learn to present yourself fully to God so that He can deal with your inner condition, motives, deeds, and plans. He will realign you and speak to you. Learn to withdraw from the ministry and then return to it to continue fulfilling God's will.

Ministry should not be the goal; fruit (visible results) should not be the goal, and don't let them steal your attention. Get away from ministry to continue fulfilling the Father's will. Once a month, withdraw yourself from everything so you can retreat with God, present yourself to Him fully, abide in His Word, pray, and worship. Start practicing this with the deeper understanding I laid out in both the book and this journal. You don't need to reinvent the wheel and struggle like

I did. I've already walked a long way and shared some of my most treasured experiences, as well as mistakes, victories, and knowledge of how everything operates in the spiritual world.

Right now, God is calling you to draw closer to Him. He wants to raise ministers after His own heart who will do His will and fulfill all His desires. The Holy Spirit doesn't force anyone. He's inviting you to draw near. If you want to be close to God and fulfill His will, learn from Jesus. When rumors about Him spread more and more, and a great multitude of people flocked to Him to hear Him and be healed of their diseases, He went to deserted places and prayed. Ministry was not His goal; the Father was. We should live like Jesus. Therefore, get away from everything, stop all the commotion, and retreat with God. It is time to start expanding yourself from within so that God can test your heart and deal with you so that there will be more of Him in your life. May your soul forever cling to God Himself.

It was Him who gave all of Himself for you. Him who adopted you and called you His son, His daughter. Him who wanted you to be born. Him who resurrected you in Christ. Him who called you by name. Him who wished to have intimacy with you. Him who gave Himself for you. It was He who died to redeem you and restore all that was lost so that you could be in His presence, His nature, and His glory.

Thank You, Jesus!!!

_____

_____

_____

_____

_____

_____

_____

_____

_____

_____

_____

_____

_____

_____

_____

_____